A
SIX
GALLERY
PRESS
BOOK

6GP

ISBN 978-0-9782961-4-8

Six Gallery Press
P.O. Box 90145
Pittsburgh, PA 15224

Email: editors@sixgallerypress.com

book design by ryan bernhardt at
moustache/moustache
ryan.bernhardt@gmail.com

POEMS

ARAB ON RADAR

Angele Ellis

Front photo: The author's grandfather, Toufic Traad Kmeid-Ellis, with unidentified companion, circa 1919.

Back photo: The author, aged six, with her brother Christopher, her aunt, Sister Ancilla, and her father, Rafic.

For my family – inherited and chosen, living and dead

The following poems first appeared in *Mizna: Prose, Poetry and Art Exploring Arab America*:

"Arab on Radar," Volume 4, Issue 2.
"Banadoura," Volume 7, Issue 2.
"The Blue State Ghazals," Volume 7, Issue 2.
"Cigar Store American," Volume 4, Issue 2.
"Federal Building," Volume 4, Issue 2.
"If We Live," Volume 7, Issue 2.

Contents

Arab on Radar

the band poster said, an accusation, a declaration of secret
identity. *Ayhrr-ub*, I hear in my grandfather's voice, then
Ahab the Ay-rab, that novelty song of the sixties where the
girlfriend whinnies like a camel – very funny – by the guy
who later sang that everyone is beautiful but I guess he made
a few exceptions. We usually said Lebanese, a measure
of blamelessness until Beirut became a synonym for Hell.
Some preferred Phoenician, ancients in merchant ships with
purple sails, anything to erase the hated word that brought
us from whiteness to darkness. It was all about whiteness.
Trying to ignore the cartoon sheiks with their huge noses
while we measured ours, praying they wouldn't get bigger.
You're not Lebanese? said the bookstore clerk who recognized
the golden cedar of Lebanon around my neck. Yes, I
am. *But you're so pale!* he cried. Malcolm X had a vision of
universal brotherhood if not sisterhood on his pilgrimage to
Mecca, *hajis* in every shade from ivory to sable, but we were
Christians so that let us out. Sometimes we were taken for
Jews – ironic recognition, Semite to Semite, or just another
tired form of bigotry. My grandfather, slowly dying, speaking
to me in Arabic from his hospital bed. My aunt saying,
*Bayee, you know she doesn't understand. Your father should have taught
you,* he replied in English as heavy as a punishment. *But your
father said to me, What do I need it for?* What do I need it for
now except that the pain of denial persists like a blip on the
screen of consciousness in every war, declared or silent.

If We Live

For J.R.

to be of arab descent
is a practice of disassociation,
you write. I read *dislocation*,
wrenched identity. Hanging
limply from sorrow's shoulder.
You write, *i guess i always knew*
but it was so unconscious...
Our grandmothers counted their gold
along the lengths of their arms.
We spin ours from paper until dawn.
If someone said our true names three times,
cousin, would we flame and disappear?
as if most americans can distinguish
the differences, or even care to...
Does every desperate act erase the differences,
bring us closer to those in nameless cells
held by force of lawlessness or burning will?
If we live, John, my grandfather said
when anyone spoke of the future. If we live.

Arabic Lesson

Unlike the illiterate villager in an Arab novel
I know *alef* from a telegraph pole
single stroke of the definite article
first letter of my French name
I have chanted this alphabet from childhood
catching letters but not words
incantation of my lost culture
fractured Rosetta Stone
fever dream of our restless planet
Remember: short vowels are implied
many words are deduced from context
study the transmissions carefully
can you tell *kalb* from *qalb*, dog from heart?
Remember: *khay* is harsh yet soft
not the hard k that is actually *qof*
a q requires no u except in transliteration
which is why Koran is Qu'ran
Remember: written letters are easy to confuse
mnemonics may be necessary
The Bay of Noon reminds me
dot on the b, *bay*, submerged under the curve
dot on the n, *noon*, high like the midday sun
Remember: *shouf* means look
insistent preface to assertions
you may read as arguments
you may read as threats
Remember: there are two ways to yes
aiwa means just yes, *na'am* means I agree
even if that happens only rarely
Start here: *shouf*

Cigar Store American

What were we made on? Newspapers and cigars.
The gloom-dampened dust of Giddi's store –
ground floor of The Grand Union Hotel,
three stories of red brick, its rooms unmentionable.
Small-town prosperity raised like the flag, sunrise to sunset.
And the cigar stub, brown and pungent, in Giddi's mouth –
not the best brand, nor the worst. Stage business.
Knowing better than to blab back in 1948,
when the undercover cop bought illegal lottery tickets,
Giddi the last connection for some shadowy hood
he insisted he knew only as "Jake."
Small change, surviving on the pennies of consignment,
the dead headlines of Capone, the Lindbergh baby, FDR,
Lucky Strike Green marching off to war
and not returning. Eisenhower came in,
and the ice-cream freezer. Vietnam and *hafidi* choosing
under their father's jaded eye one comic
and one candy bar, no whining.
Giddi kept shop until the day he turned seventy-three.
His sign with the movable clock face stalled
at an unreachable hour. He discovered deafness,
a relief from years of shoptalk,
but his mouth around his stogie stayed the same.

Banadoura

You need tomato seed from the Old Country,
my grandfather said, cupping the hands of his nineties,
verdigris and ochre, a map of two continents.
Remember – I used to grow tomatoes – four, five, six pound.
Pronouncing it *bound*, as we are to our deepest dreams.
Miraculous though not as large as Cinderella's pumpkin,
New World to Old World, reified, returning –
ripening exiles, almost too heavy for the stalk.
I can't get the seed for you now, but maybe your father –
his eyes dimmed and brightened, as when he said to guests,
Come back, now that you remember the road.
Think of the tomato seed, so tough it will survive
the acid twists of the digestive tract, the science
of sewage processing – the seedlings rise stubbornly,
again and again, from treated night earth. Here
is your metaphor, the living flesh, the flavor
of pure summer back to the original Garden,
the knowledge we were meant to devour.

Mahjar

In memory of A.H.E.

The émigré became a writer,
her ink the blood of exile.
A voice cannot carry the tongue
and the lips that give it wings.
Now those wings are brittle,
drowned in idiom and dried
in translation, with ellipses.
Here I am sending you a picture…
her cracked albums of the forgotten
look at the waterfall behind me
frozen by the lens, prophetic
even if all its water would fall
on the burning fire in my heart…
it will not be enough to extinguish it.
Even if passion became rage,
a marooned mind feeding on
the white sustenance of paper.
May God show me the light of your face…
standard start to every letter,
saluting those never met again.
She surmounted seventy years of winter,
snow in drifts like unread pages.
To call my friend across the valley…
to take, taste and talk endlessly…
always the longing to go back,
made poignant by repetition.
Your pain is the breaking of the shell
that encloses your understanding.
Was her wish finally granted,
from there view the vast sea…
can a body purified by flame
find breath in memory?
All your hours are wings that beat
through space from self to self.

Kashishi

For R.G.E.

How many generations
have we been peddlers of notions,
our ribbons of battle
fluttering from *kashishi* –
livelihood out of suitcases –
from packs, from the *karra*
your father pushed ten miles
along the Black River?

Selling like a Syrian woman.
Like Aunt Christine,
dismissed at Ellis Island
(*Country of origin: Syria*
Race: Colored)
Christine, whose narrow wrists
I inherited, lifting her brother
from Mount Lebanon
with a year's iconic work.

In the formal photograph
they sent back to the home
of war and famine
her hand is on his shoulder,
proudly thickened by labor
as his hands, resting
unaccustomed at his sides.

Now with softened hands
we wind our ribbons
through a maze of notions.
Inshallah, we can do no other.

Through the Looking Glass

For C.E.

Dusty glass door with its skeleton key
becoming soft gauze, mist, *mizna*.
Scrambling through like Alice.
In my grandparents' looking glass world,
books opened backward, right to left.
No mirror image could reveal
the riddle of a jabberwocky rhyme.
A vorpal blade on the wall
outgrinned the Cheshire cat.
The Caterpillar's hookah sat unsmoked,
on the Sheep's unreachable shelf.
Its looking glass name was *narghile*.
When they used a word, it meant
just what they chose it to mean.
She the Red Queen, he the White King,
mismatched on their adjacent squares.
The game was checkers, not chess.
She was one of the thorny kind
yet he, moving twice as fast,
ended up with all the crowns.
Believing in six impossible things
for breakfast, lunch, and dinner –
we would have settled for jam
tomorrow and jam yesterday.
Living backward made us giddy.
It is only now that memory works
both ways. Which of us dreamed it –
those from the country of nights
five times as warm and as cold,
or those who turned away and woke?

June 1967

For C.M.E.

A stream of blacktop
sticky at the edges

Dark as oil
or dried blood

The raw selvage
of any suburb

Dividing us
that week of war

Our neighbor crossed
in kitten heels

One of the chosen
with a message

I'm telling you -- bring
your daughter home now

The daughter in question
the babysitter next door

Who traded American nights
for college days in Beirut

Her mother cried -- mine
hissed at the righteous back

What does she have
a hotline to Tel Aviv?

Our own telephones
sizzled with danger

We became Arabs
separated from Jews

The headlines screamed
like rockets

Of our losses
and incompetence

While bombs fell
near someone I knew

There were no soldiers
on Sparton Lane

Just secrets
gnawing inside

As in the fable
Mother told us

The stoic Spartan boy
who bled to death

Rather than surrender
his forbidden fox

The murderer he hid
beneath his shirt

Reading the Cup

Unfathomed, the deep blue sea
is black and bitter – Arabic coffee
boiled three times in a copper pot.
Drink to the silted grounds
in heart-scalding gulps.
Turn your cup over.
Fate will drip downward,
settling in cloud-negatives.
Believe me when I say:
I read what I see in the cup.
Rock, paper, scissors.
You will build a home,
receive the news you long for,
cut short your bad luck.
To scry is to be seer and sieve,
straining hope into each sign.
How else could we bear
to gaze into the dark?

Byblos

For D.T.E.

By the flashing Mediterranean
that bluest eye
students sprawled against
ancient stones are singing:
Smoke on the water
a fire in the sky.
Deep purple dreams,
the color of Phoenician dye.

So many soundings
before we touch bottom –
prizing the wrecks,
impounding what we seize.
Beneath the Crusader castle
(pocked with green pillars
that floated down the Nile)
lie fourteen civilizations.
At dry seabed, a carved pebble
with a strangely human face,
a row of fisherman's huts
no larger than monks' cells –
relics of the Canaanites,
tribute to the sea god El.

As in a fairy tale, I live
nine thousand years in one day.
Our guide waves his hand
from the battlements to say,
We are all the same people.
Once, walking this shoreline
silted with dirt from the dig
he saw in the transparent water
Roman coins – shining for him,
like they were minted yesterday.

The Beirut Ghazals, 2000

I. Arrival

Sitti's old needle, bending the quartertones.
Allo, allo, al-looo Bei-ruuut.

A song about a wrong number, a flirtation.
I'm not dark, I'm not fair, I'm medium.

We fly in the face of a travel advisory.
Turks, once oppressors, bring hot towels.

My face is ghostly in the airplane window.
Fair, like you, she said. *Medium, like your sister.*

I read about a ballplayer who despises New York.
Imagine...the 7 train to the ballpark, looking like Beirut.

II. Mountains

The grapes are unripe in our great-uncle's arbor.
Powdery as the cheeks we kiss three times in greeting.

What do Americans think of us? our cousins ask.
My heart lurches, as on the dizzying drive from the sea.

Even if I had three languages I could not capture this:
the shade of the shutters, like peacocks walking on water.

Terraced hillsides on the brink of mythic abundance.
Already the roses are bowls of unbearable sweetness.

Jouhaina the *sheikha* laughs slyly, veiled in cigarette smoke.
This is why I like it here at Kattine – no one exciting.

III. Green Line

In war photos, a ruin weathered by bullets.
Appearing more ancient that what it protected.

The Beirut Museum, split center of *al-Harb ahliya*.
In a land of ironies, East is Christian, West Muslim.

Curators prepared for eruption as if saving Pompeii.
Small treasures in bank vaults, others entombed in concrete.

Among the successes, one case of arresting failure.
Matter is transformed, even as it is destroyed.

A rainbow of Roman glass vials, fused by explosion.
Piled one on top of the other, like bodies.

IV. Qana

My cousins have not been south in twenty-five years.
Half-lives spent in the fragile keeps of the clans.

We are drawing close to the heat of the border.
We walk as if bones pricked the soles of our feet.

This could be the place where water became wine.
Now history is an accusation on a wall: *Hussayn*.

The villagers fled to the UN compound for shelter.
The Israeli howitzers scored a direct hit.

Beyond recognition: the rubble, the burnt children—
The places where blame never becomes responsibility.

V. Departure

The clerk stamps our passports, charmed by sisterhood.
Who is the oldest? he asks – *kbeir*, the bigger.

Our luggage squats on the cracked tarmac.
We point out each piece, as if that neutralized danger.

Are you afraid? The thought rolls like a prayer bead.
No – *la*, clicking my tongue in ancestral disdain.

Samarra is anywhere: death, inescapable.
A patch of black ice, a vessel bursting in the brain.

The same clerk deplanes, security check over.
Take care of your sisters, he says, smiling into my eyes.

Paris of the Middle East

7/14/06
you wake with different eyes
your history is blazing

your cousins shut their ordinary lives
your uncle folds his useless ticket
a face you glimpsed is shattered
a bridge you crossed is broken

they block the lines
but you get through to hear
darling come next summer   God willing

in Goya's Disasters of War
the artist writes on his images
Yo lo vi   I saw it
No se puede mirar   one cannot look
in scene after scene
the eyes of the dead are opened

the tears of the universe
are neither rain nor stars
they are bombs

Hyphenated Complexities

For F.Z.

Are you a full American?
asked the journalists,
counting the students
fresh off the boat
from blasted Beirut.
Uncomfortable pause
raised eyebrow
slight of hand.
Next in this
gavotte of opposites:
Why would you go there?
What did you expect?
Then the story
cut to its Procrustean lead:
Arab-Americans, Muslim-Americans
crowded belated ships
for which we tried to make them pay
held up their passports
cried out loud for their cousins
while we said they were crying for themselves.
The Man Without A Country
knew he was in exile, but what of them?
Are you a full American?
or are you —

The Blue State Ghazals

I'm crying for all the other mothers. – Cindy Sheehan

8/17/05

Humble-hearted mother, war is unkind.
Weep *on the bright splendid shroud of your son.*

I cry for the kids playing tag on the grass.
They still believe that we are free and brave.

Would thirty flickering candles make a target?
We cup our flames as tenderly as babies' heads.

Say fifteen hundred, fifteen thousand, a quarter million.
We toll the deaths and those come to mourn them.

Unity is fragile as a child's paper chain.
Doing a small thing, then dispersing into darkness.

8/20/05

At war's doorway, a man places a makeshift sign.
No Lies Told Today, Recruitment Center Has Been Shut Down.

The Fox cameraman betrays his politics, screaming:
Arrest them, they assaulted my camera.

A police dog bites the leg of a grandmother, retreating.
Pepper spray spatters a woman's glasses as she is Tasered.

Again, the air stings with outrage and involuntary tears.
Handcuffs appear, with no magician's spell to spring them.

Crimes against property will always be punished.
The invisible ink on the Bill of Rights, appearing under fire.

8/22/05

I ignore alerts as the sky changes color:
Yellow dawns, pollution-orange sunsets, bloody nights.

Is memory more than cards of identity?
Enemies are faceless, fear the mirror of the soul.

Any eye might be a lens, any vagrant a terrorist.
Safety demands we swallow everything whole.

Territories bear prints of the powerful and dying.
I want to wash all the flags instead of burning them.

Every map they show is distorted:
Our souls are gerrymandered, whorls of red and blue.

Federal Building

I enter through security as taxpayer,
the needle's eye of citizenship. Bag on the table,
keys in a plastic container that could hold mail
or explosives. The only way in and out.
I remember with strained nostalgia
the protests of the eighties –
South Africa, Nicaragua, El Salvador,
the sit-ins at congressional offices,
the time we rode up and down the elevators
with our leaflets until the guards nabbed us
and threw us out. And that last time,
the sit-in during Desert Storm,
suspended between freedom and arrest,
swimming in ether like exotic fish
while our friends pressed against the aquarium glass
with hopeful signs
as if we could change history, levitate the building
like Abbie Hoffman tried with the Pentagon.
Now we are lucky to stand unmolested
on the public sidewalk,
the thin edge of the wedge of democracy.

On Hearing That FBI Anti-Terrorism Agents Spied on the Thomas Merton Center

For M.M.R.

Pacifism is dangerous.
Thomas Merton, the Trappist monk
who rose above his Seven-Storey Mountain
to the Buddhist peaks of Nepal,
was electrocuted by a faulty fan
while visiting the Dalai Lama.
In his first and last filmed talk, he said:
Now I will disappear for a while,
and we can all go get a Coke or something.
And he did – yet reappears
when anyone relives his revelation
at Louisville's 4th and Walnut:
I suddenly saw the secret beauty of their hearts…
If only we could see each other that way
all the time. There would be no more war…
Beauty the secret missed by surveillance,
blacked out like lines in a classified file.
Unseen in those *opposed to the U.S. war in Iraq*
left-wing…advocating…many political causes
appear[ing] to be of Middle Eastern descent.
The war against terrorism makes the world blind
to Merton's radical belief that if we truly saw
we might fall down and worship each other.
Now freedom will disappear for a while,
and we can all go get a Coke or something

Allegheny County Jail

For L.E.N.

outdated by the time it was opened
witness the black-toothed gates
whimsical anachronism in 1884
to the architect H.H. Richardson

five stories of tiered cages
faced by tunneled walkways
a system austere and stern
not a panopticon/but a gauntlet
for reflection on past deeds in silence
(silence refracting the past, deedless)

arch Bridge of Sighs
linking sentence to penance
street below muddy as a Venetian canal
the Grand Tour includes torture chambers
crenellated splendor of the mythic Outside

January 1902: Mrs. Soffel, warden's wife
freed her robber lover and his brother
their bodies flayed by bullets/her punishment
release to Edwardian solitude

****

August 6, 1985: in greasepaint and ashes
mourning in both black and white
reanimating shadows of Hiroshima
we crawled through the legs
of the Rockwell security guards
leaving ghost marks on polished shoes
roar of light on the piazza/smell of the crowd
acting/not acting as we were dragged away

September: sentenced/for refusing to pay fines
we waited/backs to a peeling wall
for entrance to the mythic Inside

a sound not human but of course it was
a woman howling/piercing the stones
falling through the door/shoved by the matron
I gave you five dollars, now you have to leave
face pilled with tissue/frantic weeping
mourning in both black and white

human processing: street clothes impounded
shower a cup of delousing fluid
yellow as piss or Mountain Dew
identity one more thing drained away
as the sergeant inspected our naked selves
for tracks/wounds/scars
she said kindly: *I really hate this part*

at four o'clock dinner in our blue overalls
cutting ham with plastic spoons
sugar for the addicts/no vegetables
the other women talked about the howling one
simple/homeless/raped on the streets

jail was safety to her, not five dollars and freedom

last-minute reprieve/women's gym night
primping and giggling shushed sternly
the sergeant: *you understand these men
see women only twice a week*
not a panopticon/but a gauntlet
the Grand Tour includes torture chambers
catwalk bisecting five stories of tiered cages

the men bare-chested/clenching the bars
for reflection on past deeds in silence

our bodies flayed by stares/their punishment
being numbered and forgotten
the pent energy in each fissioning eye
sufficient to split a world

at Hiroshima, the blast printed forever
patterns of clothing on the skin beneath

****

December 2005: all calm and bright
behind the black-toothed gates
cells replaced by chambers/glass balconies
sentencing reigns/penance has moved offsite
in one corner a cage preserved/larger empty
like reconstructing a dinosaur from its skeleton
outdated by the time it was opened

not J's cell/painted like Rousseau's hothouse
flowering years after she killed the bastard
not L's/who passed bad checks/had five children
not C's/ghost-marked by miscarriage
and the drugs she stole for her lover
for reflection on past deeds in silence
(the past reflecting silence staring still)

the Bridge of Sighs whispers no more

at four o'clock dinner in our blue overalls
cutting ham with plastic spoons
sugar for the addicts/no vegetables

we never asked what was safety to them

Old Country

For L.M.E.

Start from the Old Country
land of leaden dreams
the alchemy of nightmare
It was poor there, bella

The calendar of saints
no protection from miracles
the day of the great earthquake
I saw the earth swallow a cow

The month of *l'influenza*
you watched the corpses carried
from the House of the Insane
Buried in the blankets they slept in

Dawns your mother slaved
at the bakery for *lire*
your father sent no money
His mother said, "You're lying"

When his long-awaited letter
called you to the new country
your mother clung to promise
Maybe he's changed, she said

His drinking fed his rages
the shame of broken language
the baby doomed at birth
She begged him to go back

America, America
your mother under morphine
wandering in her final hours
Then she didn't know me

Elegy for Nonna

In memory of V.G.V.

Recomposed, a version of yourself,
more care expended on appearance for this day
than for your last year in hospital.
They've given back your glasses and your teeth,
your wedding ring, your medal of the Virgin,
the cornflower blue dress worn to a grandchild's wedding.
Your pallor makes me think of a sifting of flour,
as if you'd been baking in the kitchen of memory.
You whose hands were always restless with chores,
then merely restless. Today they play cat's cradle
with a rosary. Your mouth is slightly awry.
I would say mocking, but you never mocked.
We kneel before you singly and in pairs,
awed or relieved, except for those who
look away, as from an accident.
Here and not here. Everywhere and nowhere.
You are so small you almost disappear.
One good tug and your beads would scatter
to the corners of this room – each one a keepsake,
an accusing eye. *Hail Mary, full of grace…*
Mother of all mothers, pray for us.

Humpty Dumpty

I was a happy baby, propped in a chair,
board-like brace between my legs
forcing hipbones into their sockets,
useless feet closed like shells.
I hugged a grinning Humpty Dumpty,
knowing before memory cool plastic face,
squashy barrel chest, trailing limbs
that would do him no good on walls.

He gave me a taste for strange
love objects and great falls.

I clung to him until the brace came off,
learned to walk without having crawled.
The ledge was too narrow. I toppled.
All the king's horses and all the king's men
brought stretchers and syringes,
prescriptions and library paste –
but the most perfect shape in nature
lay shattered, scrambled, fried.

Better to have waited in warm straw
for the break to come from within,
patient tapping claiming daylight
until I cast off the blind casing of beginning,
not terrified to walk, fall, walk again.

Snow Queen

The Devil's mirror, carried upward by grinning demons, shatters from delight in mocking Heaven. The splinters drift toward Earth. Whenever they pierce a human heart or eye, distortion becomes a field of desolation. To the waking wounded, every flower is a rank weed, trampled along the path to the palace of the Snow Queen. Kai disappears, traveling northward. His devoted Gerda follows.

The palace is perfection without love: wood and cloth and tile are rendered in ice, flawlessly frozen. Kai spends endless hours making geometric circles with an icicle on a sheet of rime. He cannot acknowledge Gerda. Only when she takes his insensate being in her arms and rains hot tears on his chest and eyes do the splinters dissolve, reclaiming him from the realm of rigid reason.

Dreams decked in diamonds are shards of that mirror, which must have looked beautiful descending, glowing like the face of the Angel of Light.

Gulf

The day I caddied for my father,
I mistook the rules of the game.
I thought I was to chase
the drive down the fairway,
bring it back to the first tee.
When I put it in his hand,
panting, he laughed at me.
He could have been angry,
but my devotion was comic,
like a dog that will retrieve
anything its master throws:
a stick, a stone, harsh prose.
You used to say this story rolled
my sadness up into one ball.
A pocked sphere of emotion,
the apple of your eye.
The club swings, makes the ball fly.
I run, hoping to find it or die.

Florida

lush insistence
of palm and jade

sun baking the air like bread

boredom blurring tile roofs
burnt umbra

something is always whirring

tiny rainbows
in the hidden sprinklers

time the careless hand
of a god who wastes water

The April Ghazals

I. These fragments

Pain staining her skin like shrapnel.
Mind rejecting a long intrusion.

Touch metallic, inflicting new wounds.
Unholy stigmata of awareness.

Floor slanting, door double-bolted.
The windows failed, blank as pillows.

Memory shipwrecked, half-drowned.
Every map inscribed *Here There Be Monsters*.

A fish beats against the bottom of the boat.
Its heart bursts, craving more than oxygen.

II. I have shored

She sold the ring for a wilderness.
Removed, it made a hole in the universe.

Diorama behind suffocating glass.
A small mammal among predators.

Nostrils filled with the fetor of formaldehyde.
The specimen revolting at dissection.

Human ashes scattered like seeds.
Not even hope left in the box.

Hell an absence without flames.
All fire within – lye of lies, of liars.

III. against my ruins

They said she refused to follow instructions.
Words were muffled from behind their masks.

They often spoke of her duty to God.
This is why Whitman preferred to sit with animals.

They mapped her brain with colored Rohrschachs.
Mourning became electric, red and blue.

The slain can speak under enchantment.
Why were they surprised when she contradicted them?

The magician's powers are all in distraction.
Sometimes the object never reappears.

IV. Shantiih

Love is the quickening pulse of consciousness:
Something moves, but may not be born alive.

Asclepius stands with a dog or a snake.
Which is the truer avatar of healing?

The tortured may forgive the torturer.
Racks groan under this expectation.

The will to create is not the will to control.
The will to control is not power, but constraint.

Survival means tending the detritus, dully shining
Like stars that may die before light reaches us.

The Joy of Cooking

The stage beyond redemption
is reduction.
Boiling foul rags and bones
to their essence.
Straining ordinary time
through a glaze, but darkly.

Reduction takes patience,
and it finishes you –
seasoned, you can last
for months – years,
potent yet contained.

You asked for the recipe.

Forgiveness

You tell me to give up bread for a stone. Solid, smooth, mute: no place to start a poem. You speak of pure moments – while I'm waiting, impurity will do. Knowledge trumps bliss. Cover your nakedness with fig leaves or vestments, so that exposure will have the shock of truth: brave, innocent, lewd, pitiful, beautiful. Once out of paradise, we can tame only some animals. In the peaceable kingdom, the lion lies down with the lamb, but not for long. Despite the pumice of good works, the scourge of madness, the shame remains. If I venture forgiveness, hand me a fruit pit, something that could live again, a start of mystery.

Flying Dutchman

I come to see you on the Greensburg bus –
"Gongawere" blood-red across its gunwhale,
fares clanking like chains in a tackle box.
The windows are dim portholes.
I stare ahead with the driver.
His neck is battered as a steamer trunk.
We sail along the banks of another country.
Two old hands in knotted sweaters
put in their oars to mutter:
He was gray, I tell you. Gray.
Not two hours later, he died.
You know they always go that way.
At the shuttered gas station, we dock.
The captain turns and calls my name.
Your father's fin-tailed car lurches forward.
A wreck, with you lashed to the wheel.
I never remember what comes next –
the leap to dry land, or the pull of the sea.

Tornado

The sky went green, on the verge of revelation.
Lines from an editor's pencil slashed the horizon.
Then the sound described as an oncoming train
(to me the rumble of war games at Camp Drum,
that rocked me to sleep during childhood summers).
Our car a hollow tube, moving faster,
outgunning the fierce unseen funnel.
Our eyes never once turning to each other.
Small branches struck then fell away,
slapping and slapping, making no mark.
We didn't stop until torn leaves
smothered our windshield like bandages.
We opened our doors to the disbelief of disaster.
Things change quickly in the land of love.

In Camera

The night you came back,
Victorian floors made moan.
You took your photograph,
the one I cherished through
three cities and nine houses.
A gift is always on loan.
Graven images turn hearts to stone.
Rage shuttered my optic nerve.
You left. Through a migraine filter
I focused on the naked wall, and wept.
Photographs are kept for the lie
of a moment, captive light that warms.
The college darkroom, the acid bath,
your face emerging into form.
Quicker than a flash it snared me,
for decades held us fast,
a random shot of innocence
caught once, never surpassed.

From the Dead Letter Office

Disappeared in transit
promises   pleas   secrets
white ice at the interior
Nights of the Unread
what drove Bartleby the Scrivener
to his mad silence
tracing the walls of the Tombs

I will not reach you
but you imagine this
a neon arrow blinking
here here here here
between the pulses, lightning

What enters
the whorled gateway
of your ear is nothing –
as in the game of Telephone,
each whisper
twists my message
in the act of breathing

Even four words
the only ones
that Bartleby would utter:
I prefer not to

Alteration

This dream
we don't pass through
each other
bodiless
unable to speak
I find you living
seemingly real
as the scorched tract houses
stripped trees
the room
with other refugees
your shirt is wet
poison rain or tears
I give you another
I say what I wish
You know that I love you
you nod
I sit beside you
waking as I hold your hand

Reply to Mary Oliver's "Wild Geese"

For J.M.L.

We must attempt to be good.
Walking on our knees in this wintry desert
is the objective correlative of repenting.
Letting those soft animals, our bodies,
love what they love can lead to tears
in the solitary beds we have made.
Telling about despair is a monologue
babbled before many mirages.
Yes, the world goes on despite our loneliness –
and with it your wild geese,
slicing the blue sky like a black scalpel.
The beauty of landscape is distance.
The wild geese are not calling to you.
They cry out harshly
because instinct is not enough,
because every journey is a discipline,
because no home is a given.

Monarch

Here is how they grow to spread
orange wings washed with royal purple.
They thrive on milkweed, becoming
too bitter to be swallowed as prey.
The pods leak sap when pierced –
tears from a holy statue, Elmer's glue,
what a child has to mend the breaks.
Ripped open, they seed an inverted Eden –
green eyeless animals curled like victims
against the garage wall. All this
injustice feeds the piquant power
of the monarchs, flaunting
their markings, their bite.

Wolves

You are one of them, but your coat is thin
and you sleep alone on the ground at night,
inward and half-drowsing, hearing
their rough sighs and dreaming yips
under a moon that is pure light, reflected.

In the day, you run with the pack, slightly
behind – not too much – your leg is lame
but if you lag you will be bitten in a frenzy
or left to fend for yourself in the woods.
Life is the path, running, resting.

Every loss has been suffered.
Cold is only cold, pain only pain,
loneliness a shiver at dusk as the first star appears.

Wolves are animals, although their cries
could be taken – briefly – for human,
if someone was in a cabin nearby
watching for the fire to kindle,
latching the door, closing the book,
peeling the vegetables for supper.

Nature Morte

Lying stiffly at dawn
on a Stygian eddy of carpet,
whiskers fallen, snout upward,
sniffing the air for danger too late.
Crushed brown frond at its side.
Mouth open in desperation/surprise.
Entrails spilling like red yarn
above long defenseless feet.
At the edge of the composition,
black fur over coiled muscle,
ivory fangs, narrow topaz eyes.
Curled and clean –
the claws that eviscerated
with irresistible precision.

OK

The first word I read is gone,
but the first word I wrote
flows into meaning,
like *water*
into Helen Keller's palm.

Mommy left a message
on the chalkboard:
Play quietly and be good.
I was four. For the first time
I knew the need to reply in letters,
who had never formed a word.

My O was peaked, a mountain,
my K had horizontal branches.
Yet the universal yes
(all right, all ready)
assented and ascended
to the written world.

OK, I write now, facing sorrow:
OK, OK, OK, OK.

Fahrenheit 451

Here is the ending I love:
All the books burned,
the rebels walk the woods,
outlawed syllables
welting like Braille on their tongues.
To become a book!
Whether I am to be the hero of my own life...
We can remake this movie.
Trees in leaf our lost folios,
our heads hiding volumes,
imagination the phoenix
rising from our ashes.

Gesture Is Enough to Scatter Me

I find myself
in this northern cemetery
at my grandfather's grave.

Everything is shifting
in sere terrain. The grippe
of frost that once kept those
who lay down in winter
above ground until spring
has loosened – making the stones
bow, raising the coffins
into fresh mounds of burial.

I don't have much time.
They have brought me here only
because we are so near the camp.
A martial tattoo pounds
insistently against my temples.

Despite global warming,
the wiry cortex of the tree
next to his gravestone –
blasted like the fig in the Bible –
has spattered the black granite
with fallen fruit, dead ripe.
The slab (good fortune)
lists backward, as if enjoying
this dry, endless wind.

I take the chisel
somehow in my hands,
chipping around the foreign
cursive. The banned language
comes away in one piece.
I finger its dashes and dots
like a message in Morse code.

I am allowed one thing
that fits into my pocket.

Could his name be the weapon
that will cut barbed wire –
or the scrimshaw of my occupation,
hemmed in by the rising sea?

Rub it as I will,
it releases no *jinn*.

Glossary of Arabic Words

aiwa – yes

alef – the letter a

al-Harb ahliya – the civil war (used here in reference to the Lebanese Civil War, 1975-90)

banadoura – tomato

bay – the letter b

bayee – daddy

Byblos – ancient name of the Lebanese coastal town Jbeil; from the Greek word *biblos* (of Semitic origin), meaning papyrus or scroll. Site of a major archeological dig.

ghazal – Persian word for a form of lyric poetry, from the Arabic *gazal*. The author uses the ghazal as Adrienne Rich adapted it in "The Blue Ghazals" and other poems: "...a minimum of five couplets to a ghazal, each couplet being autonomous and independent of the others. The continuity and unity flow from the associations and images playing back and forth among the couplets in any single ghazal."

giddi – grandfather

hafidi – grandchildren

haji – pilgrim traveling to Mecca

Hussayn – Hussayn ibn Ali, the grandson of the Islamic prophet Muhammad, killed at the Battle of Karbala in 680 C.E. and revered as a martyr by Shi'a Muslims. The anniversary of his death is commemorated on Ashura.

Inshallah – God willing

jinn – genie or spirit

kalb – dog

karra – cart

kashishi – suitcases from which Arab-American peddlers used to sell their wares

kbeir – bigger; sometimes used to refer to the birth order of siblings

khay – the letter k

la – no

mahjar – émigré. Used to refer to a group of Arab-American writers of the 1920s, the most famous of whom was Gibran Kahlil Gibran. In "Mahjar," the lines *A voice cannot carry the tongue and the lips that give it wings*, *Your pain is the breaking of the shell that encloses your understanding*, and *All your hours are wings that beat through space from self to self* are from Gibran's "The Prophet."

mizna – cloud of the desert

na'am – agreed; it is so

narghile – hookah or water pipe, used to smoke tobacco or hashish

noon – the letter n

qalb – heart

Qana –a town near the Lebanese border, south of Tyre; possible site of the Biblical "miracle at Cana," in which Christ turned water into wine. On April 18, 1996, in its ongoing battle with Hezbollah, Israel destroyed a United Nations compound in which villagers had taken shelter. Over a hundred people, including 52 children, were killed; over 300 were injured. On July 28, 2006, during the month-long Israeli bombing of Lebanon, Qana again was hit; the official death toll was 28 civilians killed, 13 missing.

qof – the letter q

sheikha – a title of respect given to a woman of good family; from sheikh, whose origin is "elder"

shouf – look

sitti – grandmother